Cutie Dolls
Fairies in nature

by Nachmetdinova Yuneya
or Jenoviya Art

Cutie Dolls 2

Fairies in nature

Winter

Spring

Summer

Autumn

Jenoviya Art

Jenoviya Art

Jenoviya Art

Jenoviya Art

Jenoviya Art

Jenoviya Art

Jenoviya Art

Jenoviya Art

Jenoviya Art

Jenoviya Art

Jenoviya Art

Jenoviya Art

Cutie Dolls

Nature fairies

Jenoviya Art

Test page

Join me on:

Facebook: www.facebook.com/CutieDollsArt

Instagram: www.instagram.com/jenoviyafineart

Tik tok: tiktok.com/@jenoviya_art

Youtube: www.youtube.com/channel/UCVkTgH9Hp_LOVO2BTywNkXQ

You can buy my Art here:

Etsy shop:
www.etsy.com/shop/JenoviyaArtShop

Amazon:
www.amazon.com   (then tap my Name or CutieDolls)

Patreon (monthly subscribtion):
www.patreon.com/cutieDollsArt

Share your work on:

My Facebook group:
www.facebook.com/groups/JenoviyaArtsfansgroup

Instagram with hashtag:
#jenoviyaart #jenoviyafineart #cutiedolls